James Miller

The Hieroglyphic Bible

With four hunndred illustrations

James Miller

The Hieroglyphic Bible
With four hunndred illustrations

ISBN/EAN: 9783337634803

Printed in Europe, USA, Canada, Australia, Japan

Cover: Foto ©Lupo / pixelio.de

More available books at **www.hansebooks.com**

THE
HIEROGLYPHIC
BIBLE.

WITH

FOUR HUNDRED ILLUSTRATIONS.

NEW YORK:
JAMES MILLER, Publisher,
779 BROADWAY.

MOSES.

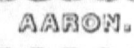

HIEROGLYPHIC BIBLE.

GENESIS I. 26.

And God said, Let us make man in our image, after our likeness, and let them have dominion over the  of the sea, and over the  of the air, and over the and over all the earth, and over every creeping thing that creepeth on the earth.

And God said, Let us make man in our image, after our likeness, and let them have dominion over the *fish* of the sea, and over the *fowl* of the air, and over the *cattle*, and over the earth, and over every creeping thing that creepeth on the earth.

GENESIS II. 22.

And the rib, which the  God had taken

from  made he a

and brought her unto

the

And the rib, which the *Lord* God had taken from *man*, made he a *woman*, and brought her unto the *man*.

GENESIS III. 1.

Now the  was

more subtle than any 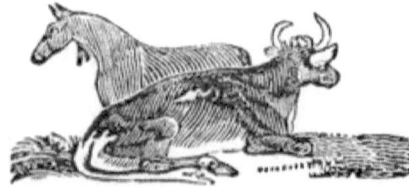 of the field

which the Lord God had made: and he said unto the

 Yea, hath God said, Ye shall not eat of every of tne garden?

Now the *serpent* was more subtle than any *beast* of the field which the Lord God had made: and he said unto the *woman*, Yea, hath God said, Ye shall not eat of every *tree* of the garden?

GENESIS III. 15.

And I will put enmity between

 and the

and between thy seed and her seed;
it shall bruise thy

 and thou shalt bruise his

And I will put enmity between *thee* and the *woman*, and between thy seed and her seed; it shall bruise thy *head*, and thou shalt bruise his *heel*.

GENESIS VIII. 9.

But the  found no rest for the sole of her  and she returned unto him into the

for the waters were on the  of the whole earth. Then he put forth his  and took her, and pulled her in unto him into the ark.

But the *dove* found no rest for the sole of her *foot*, and she returned unto him into the *ark*: for the waters were on the *face* of the whole earth. Then he put forth his *hand*, and took her, and pulled her in unto him into the ark.

10   GENESIS XIX. 16.

And while he lingered, the  laid hold upon his  and upon the hand of his wife, and upon the hand of his two  the  being merciful unto him : and they brought him forth, and set him without the city.

And while he lingered, the *men* laid hold upon his *hand*, and upon the hand of his wife, and upon the hand of his two *daughters*, the *Lord* being merciful unto him: and they brought him forth, and set him without the city.

GENESIS XXVI. 25.

And he builded an  there, and called upon the name of the 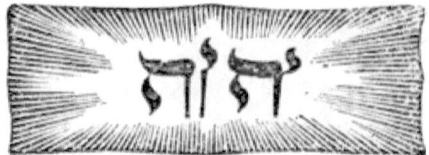 and pitched his  there; and there Isaac's servants digged a

And he builded an *altar* there, and called upon the name of the *Lord*, and pitched his *tent* there; and there Isaac's servants digged a *well*.

12   GENESIS XXXII. 5.

And I have

and  flocks, and

 servants, and

servants; and I have sent to tell my lord, that I may find grace in thy sight.

And I have *oxen*, and *asses*, flocks, and *men* servants, and *women* servants. And I have sent to tell my lord, that I may find grace in thy sight.

GENESIS XL. 11.

And Pharaoh's  was in my  and I took the  and pressed them into Pharaoh's cup, and I gave the cup into 's hand.

And Pharaoh's *cup* was in my *hand*; and I took the *grapes* and pressed them into Pharaoh's cup, and I gave the cup into *Pharaoh's* hand.

EXODUS VII. 10.

And  and  went in unto Pharaoh, and they did so as the  had commanded. And Aaron cast down his rod before  and before his servants and it became a

And *Moses* and *Aaron* went in unto Pharaoh, and they did so as the *Lord* had commanded. And Aaron cast down his rod before Pharaoh, and before his servants, and it became a *serpent*.

EXODUS XIV. 19.

And the  of God, which went before the  of Israel, removed and went behind them; and the pillar of the  went from before their face, and stood behind them.

And the *Angel* of God, which went before the *camp* of Israel, removed and went behind them; and the pillar of the *cloud* went from before their face, and stood behind them.

16 EXODUS XX. 17.

Thou shalt not covet thy neighbor's

Thou shalt not covet thy neighbor's nor his man-servant, nor his maid-servant, nor his nor his nor any thing that is thy neighbor's.

Thou shalt not covet thy neighbor's *house*, thou shalt not covet thy neighbor's *wife*, nor his man-servant, nor his maid-servant, nor his *ox*, nor his *ass*, nor any thing that is thy neighbor's.

LEVITICUS IV. 25.

And the  shall take of the blood of the sin offering with his finger, and put it upon the  of the  of burnt offering, and shall pour out his blood at the bottom of the altar of burnt offering.

And the *Priest* shall take of the blood of the sin offering with his finger, and put it upon the *horns* of the *altar* of burnt offering, and shall pour out his blood at the bottom of the altar of burnt offering.

18　　　NUMBERS XXII. 31.

Then the Lord opened the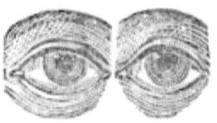

of Balaam, and he saw the

 of the

standing in the way,

and his  drawn in

his hand. And he bowed down his

 and fell flat on his face.

Then the Lord opened the *eyes* of Balaam, and he saw the *angel* of the *Lord* standing in the way, and his *sword* drawn in his hand; and he bowed down his *head* and fell flat on his face.

DEUTERONOMY V. 29.

O that there were such a  in them, that they would fear me, and keep all my  always, that it might be well with them, and with  their for ever.

O that there were such a *heart* in them, that they would fear me, and keep all my *commandments* always, that it might be well with them, and with their *children* for ever.

JOSHUA III. 16.

And as they that bare the  were come unto Jordan, and the feet of the that bare the ark were dipped in the brim of the water, for Jordan overfloweth all his banks all the time of

And as they that bare the *ark* were come unto Jordan, and the feet of the *priests* that bare the ark were dipped in the brim of the water, for Jordan overfloweth all his banks all the time of *harvest*.

JOSHUA XX. 2.

Speak to the  of Israel, saying, Appoint out for you

of refuge, whereof I spake unto you

by the  of

Speak to the *children* of Israel, saying, Appoint out for you *cities* of refuge, whereof I spake unto you by the *hand* of Moses.

JUDGES XIII. 19.

So Manoah took a 🐐 with a meat offering, and offered it 🪨 upon a unto the Lord: and the 👼 did wondrously; and 👨 and his 👩 looked on.

So Manoah took a *kid*, with a meat offering, and offered it upon a *rock* unto the Lord: and the *angel* did wondrously; and *Manoah* and his *wife* looked on.

JUDGES XIV. 18.   23

And the men of the city said unto him on the seventh day, before the  went down, What is sweeter than honey? and what is stronger than a  And he said unto them, If ye had not  with my  ye had not found out my riddle.

And the men of the city said unto him on the seventh day, before the *sun* went down, What is sweeter than honey? and what is stronger than a *lion*? And he said unto them, If ye had not *plowed* with my *heifer*, ye had not found out my riddle.

RUTH II. 7.

And she said, I pray you let me and gather after the among the so she came, and hath continued even from the morning until now, that she tarried a little in the

And she said, I pray you let me *glean* and gather after the *reapers* among the *sheaves*; so she came, and hath continued even from the morning until now, that she tarried a little in the *house*.

I SAMUEL XVII. 34.

And said unto Saul, Thy servant kept his father's and there came a and a and took a out of the flock.

And *David* said unto Saul, Thy servant kept his father's *sheep*, and there came a *lion* and a *bear*, and took a *lamb* out of the flock.

2 SAMUEL I. 6.

And the  that told him, young said, As I happened by chance upon Mount Gilboa, behold, Saul leaned upon his spear; and, lo, the  and  followed hard after him.

And the young *man* that told him said, As I happened by chance upon Mount Gilboa, behold, Saul leaned upon his spear ; and lo, the *chariots* and *horsemen* followed hard after him.

I KINGS X. 25.

And they brought  his every present,

 of silver, and vessels of gold,

and garments,  and and spices,

 and mules, a rate year by year.

And they brought every *man* his present, *vessels* of silver, and vessels of gold, and garments, and *armor*, and spices, *horses*, and mules, a rate year by year.

2 KINGS IV. 10.

Let us make a little chamber, I pray thee, on the   and let us set for him there a   and a   and a   and a   and it shall be when he cometh to us, that he shall turn in thither.

Let us make a little chamber, I pray thee, on the *wall*: and let us set for him there a *bed*, and a *table*, and a *stool*, and a *candlestick*: and it shall be, when he cometh to us, that he shall turn in thither.

1 CHRONICLES XVI. 3.

And he dealt to every one of Israel, both [man] and [woman], to every one a [loaf] of bread, and a good piece of [flesh], and a [flagon] of wine.

And he dealt to every one of Israel, both *man* and *woman*, to every one a *loaf* of bread, and a good piece of *flesh*, and a *flagon* of wine.

30   2 CHRONICLES XIV. 15.

They smote also the  of

 and carried away

 and

in abundance, and returned to Jerusalem.

They smote also the *tents* of *cattle* and carried away *sheep* and *camels* in abundance, and returned to Jerusalem.

EZRA VII. 27.   31

Blessed be the  God of our  which hath put such a thing as this in the king's  to beautify the  of the Lord which is in Jerusalem.

Blessed be the *Lord* God of our *fathers*, which hath put such a thing as this in the king's *heart*, to beautify the *house* of the Lord which is in Jerusalem.

NEHEMIAH III. 3.

But the 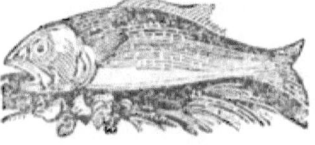 - gate did the sons of Hassenaah build, who also laid the beams thereof, and set up the  thereof, the  thereof, and the bars thereof.

But the *fish*-gate did the sons of Hassenaah build, who also laid the beams thereof, and set up the *doors* thereof, the *locks* thereof, and the bars thereof.

ESTHER VI. 8.

Let the roy-al apparel be brought which the 👑 useth to wear, and the 🐎 that the king rideth up-on, and the 👑 royal, which is set upon his head.

Let the royal apparel be brought which the *king* useth to wear, and the *horse* that the king rideth upon, and the *crown* royal which is set upon his head.

JOB IV. 17, 18.

Shall mortal man be more than God? Shall a man be more pure than his Maker? Behold, he put no trust in his and his he chargeth with folly.

Shall mortal man be more *just* than God? Shall a man be more pure than his Maker? Behold he put no trust in his *servants*, and his *angels* he chargeth with folly.

JOB XXVI. 13.

By his ⟨spirit⟩ he hath garnished the heavens;
His ⟨hand⟩ hath formed the crooked ⟨serpent⟩.

By his *spirit* he hath garnished the heavens; his *hand* hath formed the crooked *serpent*.

36   JOB XXX. 28, 29.

I went mourning without the  I stood up, and I cried in the congregation. I am a brother to

and a companion to

I went mourning without the *sun*; I stood up and cried in the congregation. I am a brother to *dragons*, and a companion to *owls*.

PSALM L. 11.   37

I know all the fowls of the mountains; and the wild beasts of the field are mine.

PSALM LXXVIII. 45, 46.

He sent divers sorts of  among them, which devoured them; and which destroyed them. He gave also their increase unto the and their labor unto the

---

He sent divers sorts of *flies* among them, which devoured them; and *frogs* which destroyed them. He gave also their increase unto the *caterpillar*, and their labor unto the *locust*.

PSALM CIV. 18, 19.

The high hills are a refuge for the

and the  for the

 He appointeth the

moon for seasons; the

knoweth his going down.

The high hills are a refuge for the *wild goats*, and the *rocks* for the *conies*. He appointeth the moon for seasons; the *sun* knoweth his going down.

PSALM CXXVIII. 3.

Thy wife shall be as a fruitful by the sides of thine thy like olive plants round about thy

Thy wife shall be as a fruitful *vine* by the sides of thy *house*; thy *children* like olive plants round about thy table.

PSALM CL. 3, 4.

Praise him with the sound of the

Praise him with the psaltery and

Praise him with the timbrel and dance:

Praise him with stringed instruments and s

Praise him with the sound of the *trumpet*:
Praise him with the psaltery and *harp*. Praise
him with the timbrel and dance: Praise him
with stringed instruments and *organs*.

PROVERBS XX. 26, 27.

A wise  scattereth the wicked, and bringeth the  over them. The spirit of man is the  of the  searching all the inward parts of the belly.

A wise *king* scattereth the wicked, and bringeth the *wheel* over them. The spirit of man is the *candle* of the *Lord*, searching all the inward parts of the belly.

PROVERBS XXVI. 3. 43

A whip for the horse, a bridle for the ass, and a rod for the fool's back.

44 ECCLESIASTES XI. 4.

He that ob-
serveth the  shall not and he that regardeth the shall not

He that observeth the *wind* shall not *sow*; and he that regardeth the *clouds* shall not *reap*.

SOLOMON'S SONG, V. 11.   45

His [head] is as the most fine gold, his locks are bushy, and black as a [raven]. His [eyes] are as the eyes of [doves] by the rivers of waters, washed with milk, and fitly set.

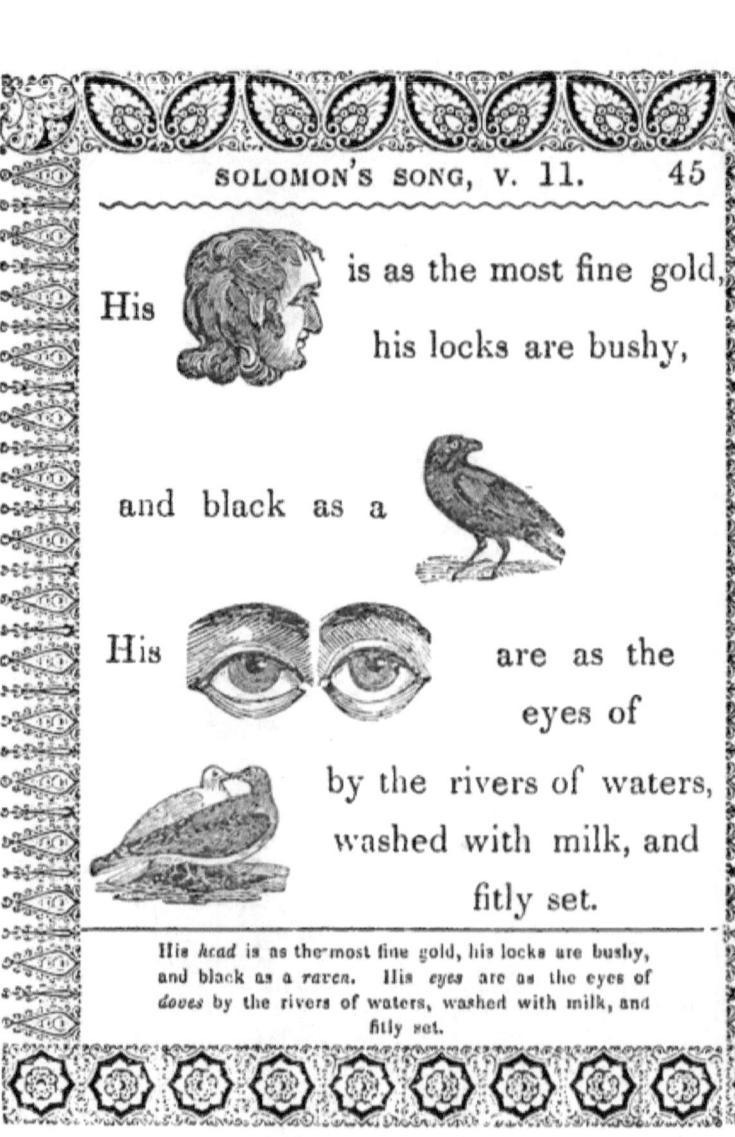

His *head* is as the most fine gold, his locks are bushy, and black as a *raven*. His *eyes* are as the eyes of *doves* by the rivers of waters, washed with milk, and fitly set.

ISAIAH VI. 6.

Then flew one of the [seraphim] unto me, having a live coal in his [hand], which he had taken with the [tongs] from off the [altar].

Then flew one of the *seraphims* unto me, having a live coal in his hand, which he had taken with the *tongs* from off the *altar*.

ISAIAH XI. 6. 47

The 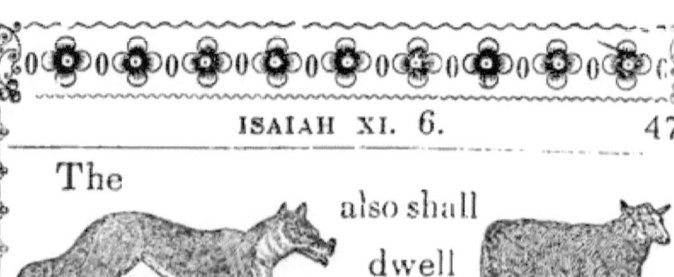 also shall dwell with the

and the  shall lie down with the

and the  and the young  and the fatling together;

and a little  shall lead them.

The *wolf* also shall dwell with the *lamb*, and the *leopard* shall lie down with the *kid*: and the *calf* and the young *lion*, and the fatling together; and a little *child* shall lead them.

Woe to them that go down to Egypt for help; and stay on  and trust in  because they are many; and in  because they are very strong; but they look not unto the Holy One of Israel, neither seek the Lord.

Woe to them that go down to Egypt for help; and stay on *horses*, and trust in *chariots*, because they are many; and in *horsemen*, because they are very strong; but they look not unto the Holy One of Israel, neither seek the Lord.

JEREMIAH XVII. 1.   49

The sin of Judah is written with a [pen] of iron, and with the point of a diamond: it is graven upon the [table] of their [heart], and upon the [horns] of your altars.

The sin of Judah is written with a *pen* of iron, and with the point of a diamond : It is graven upon the *table* of their *heart*, and upon the *horns* of your altars.

50 — LAMENTATIONS II. 4.

He hath bent his  like an enemy: He stood with his right hand as an adversary, and slew all that were pleasant to the eye in the tabernacle of the daughter of Zion: He poured out his fury like fire.

He hath bent his *bow* like an enemy: He stood with his right hand as an adversary, and slew all that were pleasant to the *eye* in the tabernacle of the *daughter* of Zion: He poured out his fury like *fire*.

EZEKIEL I. 10.

As for the likeness of their faces, they four had the of a man, and the face of a  on the right side;

and they four had the face of an  on the left side: they four also had the face of an

> As for the likeness of their faces, they four had the *face* of a man and the face of a *lion* on the right side; and they four had the face of an *ox* on the left side; they four also had the face of an *eagle*.

DANIEL VI. 5.

Then said these  We shall not find any occasion against this except we find it against him concerning the law of his God.

Then said these *men*, We shall not find any occasion against this *Daniel*, except we find it against him concerning the law of his God.

HOSEA XIII. 8.

I will meet them as a 🐻 that is bereaved of her whelps, and will rend the caul of their ♥ and there will I devour them like a 🦁

The wild beast shall tear them.

I will meet them as a bear that is bereaved of her whelps, and will rend the caul of their heart, and there will I devour them like a lion. The wild beast shall tear them.

JOEL II. 10.

The  shall quake before them; the  shall trem-ble: the  and the  shall be dark, and the  shall withdraw their shining.

The *earth* shall quake before them; the *heavens* shall tremble; the *sun* and the *moon* shall be dark, and the *stars* shall withdraw their shining.

AMOS III. 12.

Thus saith the Lord, As the shepherd taketh out of the mouth of the 🦁 two 🦵 or a piece of an 👂 so shall the children of Israel be taken out that dwell in Samaria in the corner of a bed, and in Damascus in a 🛏.

Thus saith the Lord, As the shepherd taketh out of the mouth of the *lion* two *legs*, or a piece of an *ear*, so shall the children of Israel be taken out that dwell in Samaria in the corner of a bed, and in Damascus in a *couch*.

OBADIAH I. 4.

Though thou exalt thyself as the *eagle*, and though thou set thy *nest* among the *stars*, thence will I bring thee down, saith the *Lord*.

JONAH I. 4.

But the  sent out a great into the sea, and there was a mighty tempest in the so that the was like to be broken.

But the *Lord* sent out a great *wind* into the sea, and there was a mighty tempest in the *sea*, so that the *ship* was like to be broken.

MICAH III. 11.

The  thereof judge for reward, and the thereof teach for hire, and the thereof divine for money: yet will they lean upon the Lord, and say, Is not the Lord among us? none evil can come upon us.

The *heads* thereof judge for reward, and the *priests* thereof teach for hire, and the *prophets* thereof divine for money: yet will they lean upon the Lord, and say, Is not the Lord among us? none evil can come upon us.

NAHUM III. 2.

The noise of a whip, and the noise of the rattling of the wheels, and of the prancing of horses, and of the jumping chariots.

HABAKKUK I. 13.

Thou art of purer  than to behold evil, and canst not look on iniquity; wherefore lookest thou upon them that deal treacherously, and holdest thy  when the wicked devoureth the  that is more  than he?

Thou art of purer *eyes* than to behold evil, and canst not look on iniquity; wherefore lookest thou upon those who deal treacherously, and holdest thy *tongue* when the wicked devoureth the *man* that is more *righteous* than he?

ZEPHANIAH II. 6.

And the sea coast shall be dwellings and cottages for shepherds, and folds for flocks.

HAGGAI II. 6.

For thus saith the  of Hosts, Yet once, it is a little while, and I will shake the and the and the and the dry land.

For thus saith the *Lord* of Hosts, Yet once, it is a little while, and I will shake the *heavens*, and the *earth*, and the *sea*, and the dry land.

ZECHARIAH XIV. 15.

And so shall be the plague of the  of the  of the  and of the and of all the beasts that shall be in these  as this plague.

And so shall be the plague of the *horse*, of the *mule*, of the *camel*, and of the *ass*, and of all the beasts that shall be in these *tents*, as this plague.

MALACHI IV. 2.

But unto you that fear my name shall  the of arise with healing in his and ye shall go forth, and grow up as of the stall.

But unto you that fear my name shall the *sun* of *righteousness* arise with healing in his *wings*; and ye shall go forth, and grow up as *calves* of the stall.

MATTHEW I. 20.

But while he thought on these things, behold the  of the Lord appeared unto him in a dream, saying, thou son of fear not to take unto thee Mary thy wife; for that which is conceived in her is of the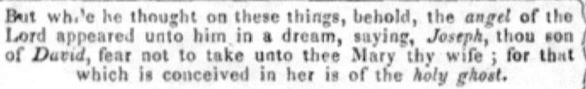

But while he thought on these things, behold, the *angel* of the Lord appeared unto him in a dream, saying, *Joseph*, thou son of *David*, fear not to take unto thee Mary thy wife; for that which is conceived in her is of the *holy ghost*.

MATTHEW III. 12.

Whose  is in his and he will throughly purge his floor, and gather his into the But he will burn up the chaff with unquenchable

Whose fan is in his hand, and he will throughly purge his floor, and gather his wheat into his garner; but he will burn up the chaff with unquenchable fire.

MATTHEW VIII. 20.

And   saith unto him,
The   have holes, and the
          of the air have nests;
but the   hath not where
Son of   to lay his head.

And *Jesus* saith unto him, The *foxes* have holes, and the *birds* of the air have nests; but the Son of *man* hath not where to lay his head.

MATTHEW x. 16.

Behold I send you forth as [sheep] in the midst of [wolves] Be ye therefore wise as [serpents] and harmless as [doves]

Behold, I send you forth as *sheep* in the midst of *wolves*. Be ye therefore wise as *serpents* and harmless as *doves*.

MARK III. 9.

And  spake

to his  that a small

 should wait on him because of the multitude.

And *Christ* spake to his *disciples*, that a small *ship* should wait on him because of the multitude, lest they should throng him.

MARK VII. 28.

And she answered and said unto him,

Yes,

yet the

under the  eat of

the  crumbs.

And she answered and said unto him, Yes, *Lord*; yet the *dogs* under the *table* eat of the *children's* crumbs.

LUKE III. 9.

And now  is laid unto the also the root of the trees;

Every therefore which bringeth not forth

good  is

and cast into the

And now also the *axe* is laid unto the root of the trees; every *tree* therefore which briugeth not forth good *fruit* is *hewn down*, and cast into the *fire*.

72 LUKE XVIII. 33.

And they shall scourge him, and put him to

And the third day he shall

again.

And they shall scourge him, and put him to *death*: And the third day he shall *rise* again.

73

LUKE XIX. 38.

Saying, Blessed be the ★ that cometh in the name of the יהוה ★ in heaven, and glory in the highest.

Saying, Blessed be the *King* that cometh in the name of the *Lord:* *Peace* in heaven, and glory in the highest.

JOHN II. 14.

And found in the  those that sold and and and the of money sitting.

And found in the *temple* those that sold *oxen*, and *sheep*, and *doves*, and the *changers* of money sitting.

JOHN III. 5. 75

 answered, Verily, verily,

I say unto thee, except a

be born

of

and of  he

the cannot

enter into the kingdom of God.

Jesus answered, Verily, verily, I say unto thee, Except a man be born of *water* and of the *Spirit*, he cannot enter into the kingdom of God.

JOHN x. 12.

But he that is a hireling, and not the 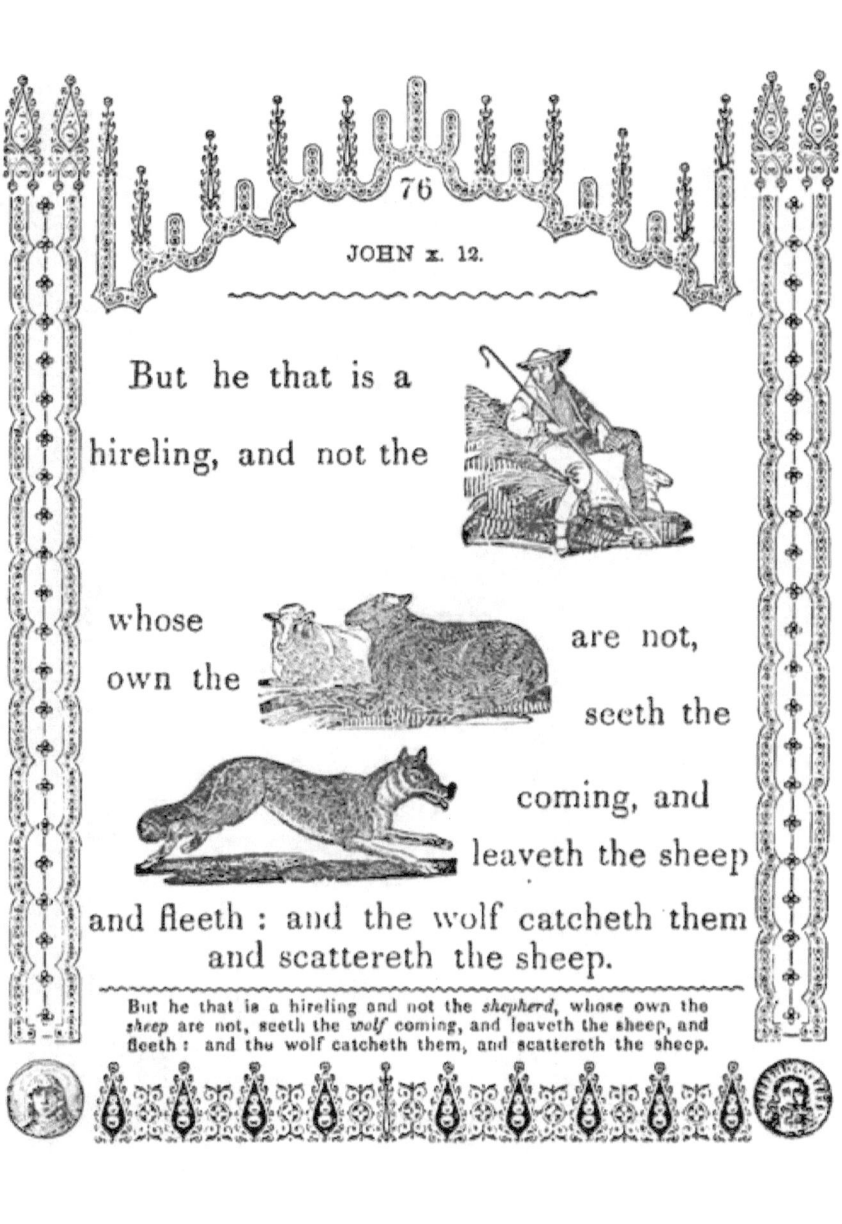 whose own the are not, seeth the coming, and leaveth the sheep and fleeth : and the wolf catcheth them and scattereth the sheep.

But he that is a hireling and not the *shepherd,* whose own the *sheep* are not, seeth the *wolf* coming, and leaveth the sheep, and fleeth : and the wolf catcheth them, and scattereth the sheep.

ACTS I. 20.

For it is written in the [book] of Psalms, Let his [habitation] be desolate, and let no man dwell therein: and his [bishop]rick let another take.

For it is written in the *book* of Psalms, Let his *habitation* be desolate, and let no man dwell therein: and his *bishop*rick let another take.

ACTS II. 25.

For  speaketh concerning him,

I foresaw the  always before my  For he is on my right  that I should not be moved.

For *David* speaketh concerning him, I foresaw the *Lord* always before my *face*; for he is on my right *hand*, that I should not be moved.

And daily in the *temple*, and in every *house*, they ceased not to teach and *preach Jesus Christ*.

80　　　　　ACTS XI. 6.

Upon the which when I had fastened mine  I considered, and saw four-footed of the earth, and wild beasts, and and of the air.

Upon the which when I had fastened my *eyes*, I considered, and saw four-footed *beasts* of the earth, and wild beasts, and *creeping things*, and *fowls* of the air.

ACTS XIV. 13. 81

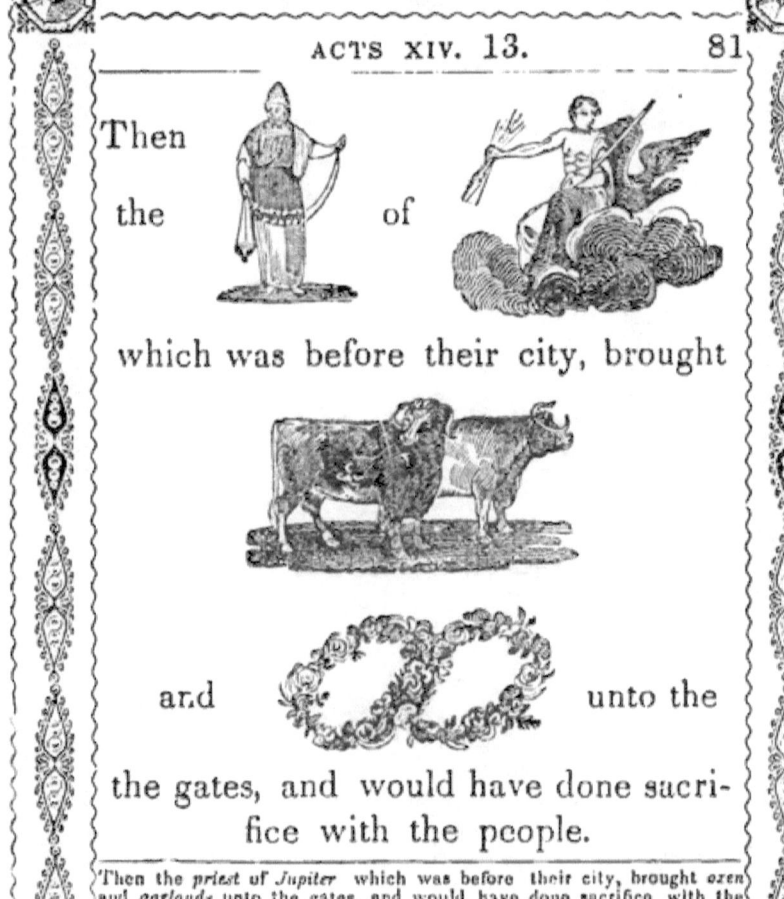

Then the [priest] of [Jupiter] which was before their city, brought [oxen] and [garlands] unto the the gates, and would have done sacrifice with the people.

Then the priest of Jupiter which was before their city, brought oxen and garlands unto the gates, and would have done sacrifice with the people.

ACTS xxvii. 30

And the shipmen were about to flee out of the  when they had let down the boat into the sea under color as though they would have cast anchor out of the foreship.

And as the shipmen were about to flee out of the *ship*, when they had let down the *boat* into the sea, under color as though they would have cast *anchor* out of the foreship.

ROMANS v. 17.

For if by one man's offence, Death reigned by one; much more they which receive abundance of grace, and of the gift of righteousness, shall reign in life by one, Jesus Christ.

ROMANS XI. 9.

And [David] saith, Let their [table] be made a [snare] and a [trap] and a stumbling block, and a recompense unto them.

And *David* saith, Let their *table* be made a *snare*, and a *trap*, and a stumbling-block, and a recompense unto them.

ROMANS XV 13.

Now the God of [figure] fill you with all joy and [figure] in believing, that ye may abound in hope, through the power of the [figure]

Now the God of *hope* fill you with all joy and *peace* in believing, that ye may abound in hope, through the power of the *holy ghost.*

1 CORINTHIANS IV. 9.

For I think that God hath set forth us the Apostles last, as it were appointed to death; for we are made a spectacle unto the world, and to angels and to men.

I CORINTHIANS IX. 9.

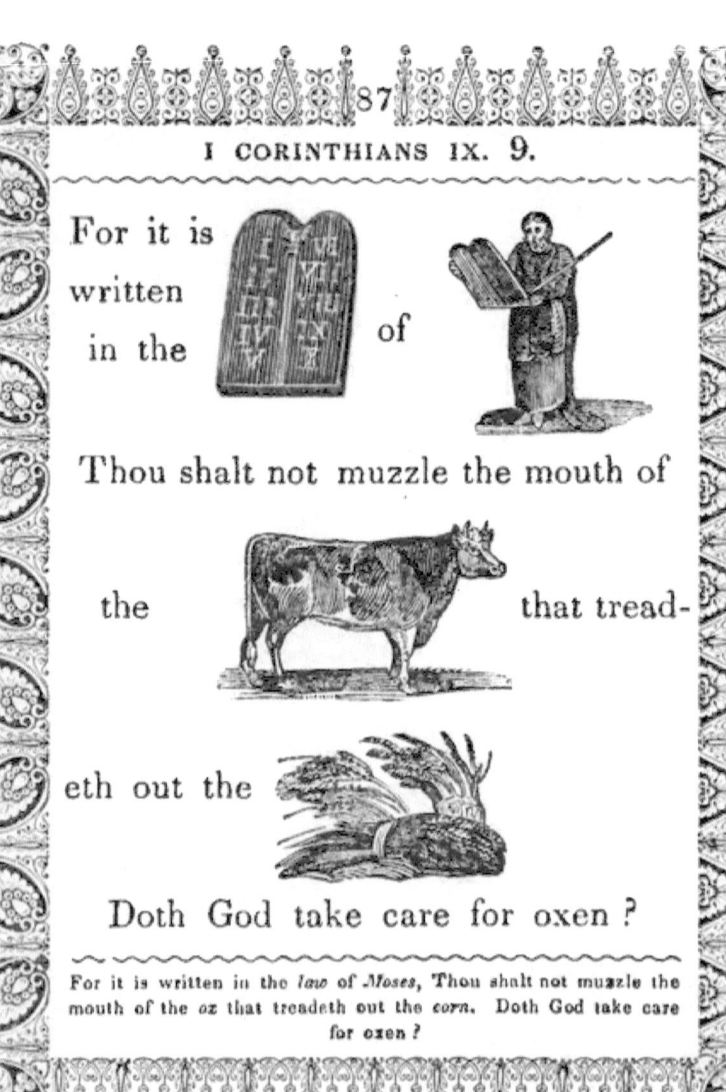

For it is written in the [tablets] of [Moses] Thou shalt not muzzle the mouth of the [ox] that treadeth out the [corn]. Doth God take care for oxen?

For it is written in the *law* of *Moses*, Thou shalt not muzzle the mouth of the *ox* that treadeth out the *corn*. Doth God take care for oxen?

2 CORINTHIANS V. 1.

For we know, that if our earthly

of this tabernacle were dissolved, we have a building of God, a house not

made with

eternal in the

For we know that if our earthly *house* of this tabernacle were dissolved, we have a building of God, a house not made with *hands*, eternal in the *heavens*.

GALATIANS VI. 7.

Be not deceived; God is not mocked: for whatsoever a 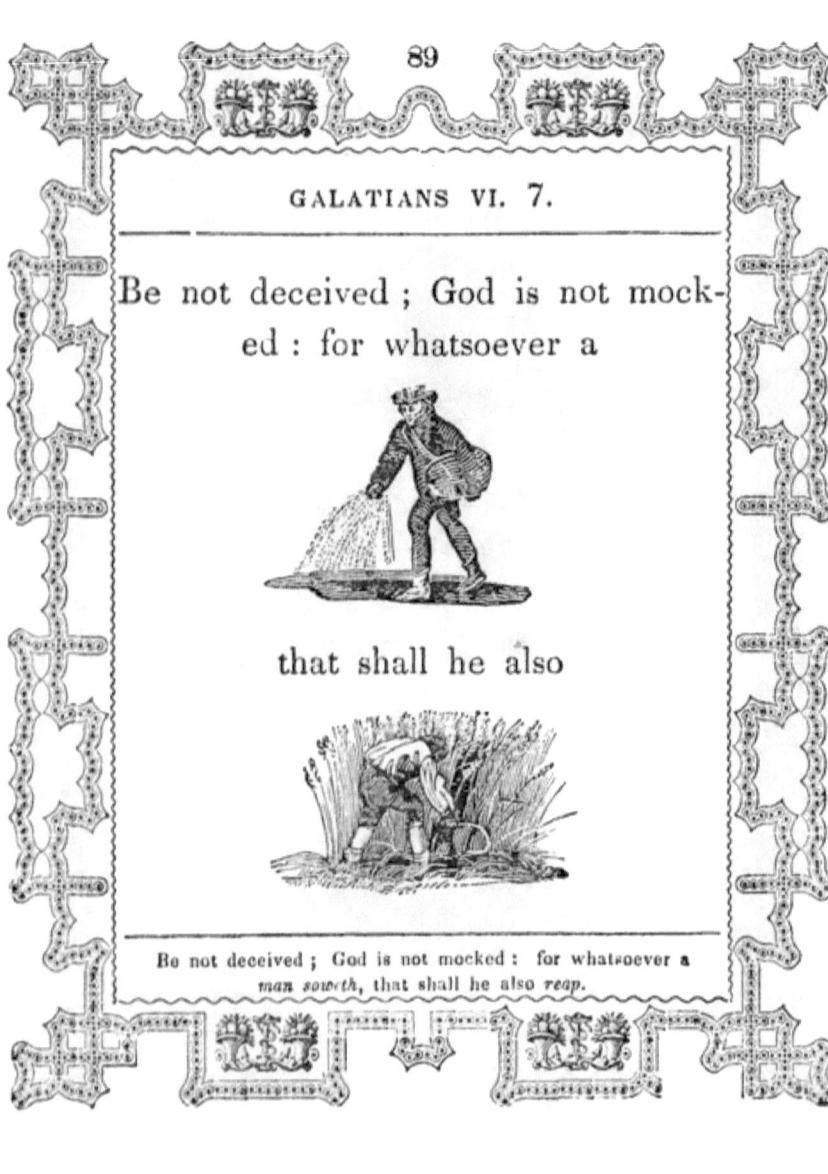 that shall he also

Be not deceived; God is not mocked: for whatsoever a *man soweth*, that shall he also *reap*.

EPHESIANS III. 17.

That ⟨Christ⟩ may dwell in your ⟨hearts⟩ by faith; that ye, being rooted and grounded in ⟨love⟩.

That *Christ* may dwell in your *hearts* by faith; that ye, being rooted and grounded in *love.*

PHILIPPIANS IV. 3.

And I intreat thee also, true  fellow, help those  which labored with me in the gospel, with Clement also, and with other my fellow-laborers, whose names are in the  of

And I intreat thee also, true *yoke*-fellow, help those *women*, which labored with me in the gospel, with Clement also, and with other my fellow-laborers, whose names are in the *book* of *life*.

COLOSSIANS I. 20.

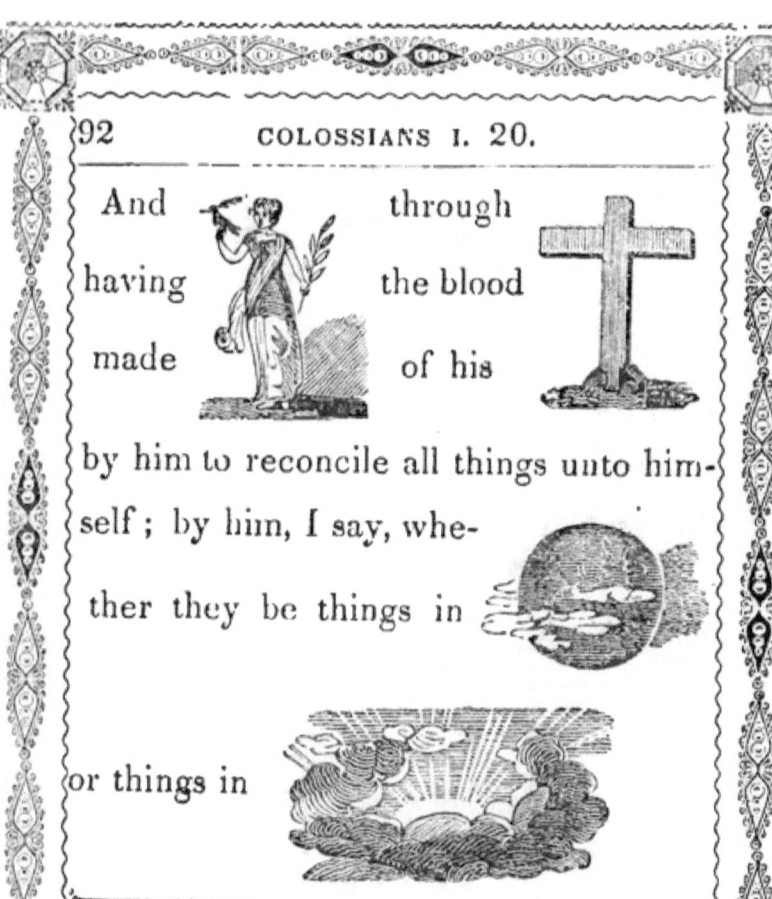

And having made through the blood of his by him to reconcile all things unto himself; by him, I say, whether they be things in or things in

And having made *peace* through the blood of his *cross*, by him to reconcile all things unto himself; by him, I say, whether they be things in *earth*, or things in *heaven*.

THESSALONIANS IV. 16.

For the  himself shall descend from heaven with a shout, with the voice of the arch-  and with the  of God: and the dead in  shall rise first.

For the *Lord* himself shall descend from heaven with a shout, with the voice of the arch-*angel*, and with the *trump* of God: and the dead in *Christ* shall rise first.

2 THESSALONIANS I. 3.

We are bound to thank God always

for you  as it is

meet, because that your

groweth exceedingly, and the

 of every one of you all toward each other aboundeth.

We are bound to thank God always for you, *brethren*, as it is meet, because that your *faith* groweth exceedingly, and the *charity* of every one of you all toward each other aboundeth.

95
1 TIMOTHY, III. 5.

For if a  know not how to rule his own how shall he take care of the of God?

For if a *man* know not how to rule his own *house*, how shall he take care of the *church* of God?

96   2 TIMOTHY, IV. 11.

Only 🐂👤 is with me Take 🦁📚 and bring him with thee; for he is profitable to me for the 🏛️

Only *Luke* is with me Take *Mark* and bring him with thee, for he is profitable to me for the *ministry*.

TITUS III. 5.

Not by works of  which we have done, but according to his mercy  saved us, by the washing of regeneration, and renewing of the

Not by works of *righteousness* which we have done, but according to his mercy *he* saved us, by the washing of regeneration, and renewing of the *Holy Ghost.*

PHILEMON, VER. 9.

Yet, for love's sake, I rather beseech thee, being such an one as Paul the aged, and now also a prisoner of Jesus Christ.

HEBREWS IX. 19.   99

For when  had spoken every precept to all the people according to the law, he took the blood of  and of  with water, and scarlet wool, and hyssop, and sprinkled both the  and all the people.

For when *Moses* had spoken every precept to all the people according to the law, he took the blood of *calves* and of *goats*, with water, and scarlet wool, and hyssop, and sprinkled both the *book* and all the people.

JAMES III. 7.

For every kind of  and of ⬚ and of ⬚ and of things in the sea, is tamed, and hath been tamed of mankind.

For every kind of *beasts*, and of *birds*, and of *serpents*, and of things in the sea, is tamed, and hath been tamed of mankind.

1 PETER II. 25.

For ye were as going astray; but are now returned unto the and of your souls.

For ye were as *sheep* going astray; but are now returned unto the *Shepherd* and *Bishop* of your souls.

I JOHN III. 10.

In this the  of God are manifest, and the of the

Whosoever doeth not righteousness is not of God, neither he that loveth not his brother.

In this the *children* of God are manifest, and the *children* of the *devil*. Whosoever doeth not righteousness is not of God, neither he that loveth not his brother.

2 JOHN, ver. 3.

Grace be with you, mercy and from God the Father, and from the the Son of the Father, in truth and love.

Grace be with you, mercy and *peace* from God the Father, and from the *Lord Jesus Christ*, the Son of the Father, in truth and love.

3 JOHN, VER. 6.

Which have borne witness of thy  before the whom if thou bring forward on their journey, after a godly sort, thou shalt do well.

Which have borne witness of thy *charity* before the *church*: whom, if thou bring forward on their journey after a godly sort, thou shalt do well.

JUDE, VER. 9.

Yet Michael the arch- when contending with the he disputed about the body of durst not bring against him a railing accusation, but said, The rebuke thee.

Yet Michael the arch *angel*, when contending with the *devil*, he disputed about the body of *Moses*, durst not bring against him a railing accusation, but said, The *Lord* rebuke thee.

REVELATIONS XIII. 2.

And the beast which I saw was like unto a 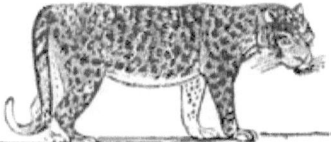 and his feet were as the feet of a  and his mouth as the mouth of a  and the  gave him his power, and his seat, and great authority.

And the beast which I saw was like unto a *leopard*, and his feet were as the feet of a *bear*, and his mouth as the mouth of a *lion*; and the *dragon* gave him his power, and his seat, and great authority.

www.ingramcontent.com/pod-product-compliance
Lightning Source LLC
Chambersburg PA
CBHW020152170426
43199CB00010B/1007